GW01237763

Adam's bike
and
Is this your hat

Hannie Truijens

Illustrated by Annabel Spenceley

Is this your hat   page 2

Adam's bike   page 10

Nelson

Is this your hat

Helen found a hat in the
road and put it on.
I don't like it, she said.

She went down the road and
met Mrs Green.
Is this your hat, said Helen.
I found it in the road.

3

No dear, said Mrs Green.

This is my hat.

Oh yes, said Helen.

Goodbye Mrs Green.

She went down the road and
met Mr Brown.
Is this your hat, said Helen.
I found it in the road.

No dear, said Mr Brown.

This is my hat.

Oh yes, said Helen.

Goodbye Mr Brown.

She went down the road and
met Mr Jones.
Is this Dobbin's hat, said
Helen.
I found it in the road.

No dear, said Mr Jones.

This is Dobbin's hat.

Oh yes, said Helen.

Goodbye Mr Jones and Dobbin.

She went down the road and
into the field.
This must be your hat, said
Helen.
Goodbye.

Adam's bike

Adam wanted a bike for his birthday.
I wish, I wish, I wish I had a bike, he said.

Mum came into his room.

Happy birthday Adam, she said.

Look under the bed.

Adam looked under the bed and
found a letter.
Look in the cupboard, it said.

12

He looked in the cupboard and
found a letter.
Look in the attic, it said.

He looked in the attic and
found a letter.
Look in the garden, it said.

He looked in the garden and
found a letter.
Look in the shed, it said.
He looked in the shed.

He found his present.

It was a bike.

Look out, said Adam.

Here I come.

I wished and wished for a bike.

And now I have one.